Adriana Crespo

Multimedia as an information resource for cancer clients

AF154753

Adriana Crespo

Multimedia as an information resource for cancer clients

Information resource for long-term central
venous catheters for clients undergoing
chemotherapy

ScienciaScripts

Imprint

Any brand names and product names mentioned in this book are subject to trademark, brand or patent protection and are trademarks or registered trademarks of their respective holders. The use of brand names, product names, common names, trade names, product descriptions etc. even without a particular marking in this work is in no way to be construed to mean that such names may be regarded as unrestricted in respect of trademark and brand protection legislation and could thus be used by anyone.

Cover image: www.ingimage.com

This book is a translation from the original published under ISBN 978-620-2-19312-2.

Publisher:
Sciencia Scripts
is a trademark of
Dodo Books Indian Ocean Ltd. and OmniScriptum S.R.L publishing group

120 High Road, East Finchley, London, N2 9ED, United Kingdom
Str. Armeneasca 28/1, office 1, Chisinau MD-2012, Republic of Moldova, Europe
Printed at: see last page
ISBN: 978-620-7-26979-2

SUMMARY

SUMMARY:

Multimedia as an information resource about long-term central venous catheters for clients undergoing chemotherapy.

Objective: To survey the strategies used by nurses to provide guidance on the Totally Implanted Central Venous Catheter (TIC-CV) for chemotherapy patients; To identify the patient's doubts about the TIC-CV: To develop a multimedia as an information resource about the (CVC-TI) for clients undergoing chemotherapy; Method: Exploratory study in which 20 nursing consultations were followed up in a chemotherapy outpatient clinic, always before starting chemotherapy treatment, in an exclusive consultation with a nurse specializing in oncology with mastery of the subject. Patients' doubts and the resources used by the nurse were observed. Results: Categorization of questions, elaboration of reasoned answers, creation of a script, storyboard where the main themes addressed were the nature of the CVC-TI and its location, questions about pain and specific care. Elaboration of a 6-minute piece of media Discussion: The core of this multimedia is visual information, non-verbal reading which can act as a mechanism for the production of meanings integrated with other fields of knowledge, and on the general culture of the individual. It represents a link between communication and knowledge, between what is seen and what is retained, between what is retained and what is expressed, between what is expressed and what is expected to be seen, guaranteeing greater understanding of the message. Conclusion: It is possible to assume that the material carefully prepared here will facilitate the patient's understanding and the nurse's informational work. It can be accessed free of charge and is a useful public resource.

Keywords: Totally Implanted Catheter Guidance; Patient Guidance Multimedia; Totally Implanted Catheter and Chemotherapy.

I - INTRODUCTION

Cancer is a global public health problem that affects children, adults and the elderly in both developed and developing countries. Its diagnosis is extremely devastating for the patient/client and family, as for many centuries it has been synonymous with mutilation, pain, fear, anxiety and death. However, therapeutic and healing possibilities have been increasing in recent decades. One of the main therapeutic modalities for treating cancer is antineoplastic chemotherapy, which can be administered, depending on each case, as the only treatment, or as a complement to surgical interventions or radiotherapy. Treatment with antineoplastic chemotherapy is based on the use of chemical agents, alone or in combination, with the aim of treating malignant tumors (PHILLIPS, 2001).

Although chemotherapeutic agents are currently available for oral use, the main route of administration is still intravenous. Many of these antineoplastic chemotherapy drugs have vesicant, vascular irritant or direct toxicity potential, thus causing aggression and inflammatory reaction of the vascular endothelium. This can evolve into sclerosis of the vessel, with loss of function caused by post-inflammatory fibrosis or even necrosis in cases of extravasation (FROEHNER JÛNIOR, 2005).

Therefore, a crucial aspect in the treatment of patients who have to undergo prolonged intravenous therapy is the presence of adequate and safe vascular access. The constant use of the superficial venous network, which is usually done by puncture using needles and polyethylene catheters, often for short-term use of isosmolar solutions and non-caustic medications, invariably leads to exhaustion of this venous system, generating intrinsic limitations such as venous sclerosis, peripheral phlebitis and extravasation, which makes it extremely difficult to visualize and puncture over the long term. This is exacerbated by the need to use hyperosmolar or vesicant solutions for prolonged periods, despite an adequate superficial venous network at the start of treatment (FROEHNER JÛNIOR, 2005).

In oncology, the use of peripheral catheters is progressively giving way to long-term venous catheters. The constant use of the venous network and the capillary fragility resulting from the disease and treatment lead to increasingly serious problems in visualizing and puncturing the blood vessel (FERREIRA, CAPONERO E TEIXEIRA 2008).

A catheter can be recommended from the start of systemic intravenous treatment. After a careful assessment of the access associated with the type of medication and duration of applications required for the planned intravenous treatment. The insertion of a fully implanted catheter is an essential part of cancer treatment for some patients. It is often the only way to access chemotherapy medication in the body. The whole process, from choosing the most suitable catheter for the patient's anatomy, preoperative examinations, the surgery itself and finally the post-operative period, must be surrounded by care so that it is as non-aggressive as possible for the patient (BRUZI E MENDES, 2011).

^ PROFESSIONAL CAREER AND PROBLEMATIZATION

My experience with patients with various types of cancer has enabled me to handle different catheters for the purpose of infusing specific drugs for their treatment. My first experience of treating cancer patients was in 1992 in an Oncology Intensive Care Unit, caring for individuals treated for various types of cancer, mainly in the post-operative period of cancer surgeries.

In 1995, I took part in the opening of a specific sector for bone marrow transplants, where I came into contact with high-dose chemotherapy for this situation. Shortly afterwards, I had contact with cancer patients in the various stages of their illness and, by accompanying internships for both undergraduate and graduate students, as well as postgraduates, I realized how essential it is for nurses to know how to properly assess the possibility of accessing vessels in a position to receive the drugs that will be infused for chemotherapy treatment. Since then, I have seen that safe venous access is essential for cancer treatment. There are currently numerous devices on the market that meet the needs of each chemotherapy treatment.

In 2007, I started working exclusively in the outpatient chemotherapy sector, where the venous devices used for chemotherapy infusion are mostly peripheral or fully implanted catheters (CVC-TI). The choice of device will depend on a number of variables, such as factors related to the disease, treatment planning and forecasting, as well as the type of medication used and the patient's capacity for self-care.

Therefore, the choice of a safe venous access becomes imperative and primordial for this therapeutic proposal to be effective and efficient.

In 2009, I set up the Nursing Consultation at the chemotherapy outpatient clinic, where the patient is systematically examined and oriented for at least two days before starting treatment. This is vital for the nurse to ascertain the best conditions for implanting or not implanting a venous catheter.

The experience of the consultation made it possible, above all, to observe that there is a difficulty for patients in understanding specifically about the implantation of the catheter in their vein, as well as the nurse's difficulty in conveying this message in a calm and positive manner. Despite the adoption of some strategies aimed at communicating with the patient, such as the use of pictures, demonstrating the device and explaining the procedure itself, many patients still don't feel satisfied and manifest a variety of behaviors, such as anxiety and worry about what will be done as part of

4

their treatment. Many then refuse to have a vessel punctured in order to place the catheter, thus delaying any proposed treatment.

Therefore, the problem and phenomenon of this project lies in patient orientation, and for effective and efficient communication about the proposed insertion of a long-term central venous catheter, aimed at the treatment of cancer patients undergoing chemotherapy, I propose the creation of a multimedia.

^ THE OBJECT OF STUDY

Interactive media as an information resource about long-term central venous catheters for clients undergoing chemotherapy.

^ THE GUIDING QUESTIONS

1- What information strategies do nurses use during nursing consultations to guide patients through the use of long-term central venous catheters during chemotherapy?

2- What questions do patients have about using a long-term central venous catheter during chemotherapy?

^ THE OBJECTIVES:

CENTRAL: To develop an interactive multimedia as an information resource about long-term central venous catheters for clients undergoing chemotherapy;

SPECIFIC:

- To describe the information strategies used by nurses to provide guidance on long-term central venous catheters for chemotherapy patients;

- Analyze patients' doubts about long-term central venous catheters.

^ JUSTIFICATION AND RELEVANCE

In systemic chemotherapy treatment, the implantation of a central venous catheter can be extremely important in creating a permanent access route. It is essential that patients understand the importance of this device for their treatment, and that a trained team accompanies and acts directly with quality care, meeting the real needs of patients and their families and avoiding complications in the use of the central venous catheter, A multimedia presentation will make it possible to clarify possible doubts, bringing greater guarantees of the patient's adherence and acceptance and less fragility and stress during antineoplastic treatment because they feel more welcome and can count on competent professionals, aiming to prevent complications generated by the manipulation and maintenance of the fully implanted central venous catheter.

II - THEORETICAL BACKGROUND

^**The** New Information and Communication Technologies (NICTs) in the world.

Image studies in their various forms, content, film, video and photography, have contributed greatly to the transmission of information in the various areas of human knowledge, whether as a source of documentation, research or as a tool for social, political and cultural intervention. This facility has brought the more technical areas of knowledge closer to the health area, specifically nursing, which is faced with a diversity of clients who need care and guidance to maintain their health or understand treatment processes.

The use of technology to facilitate the transmission of important information has been expanding in the field of nursing. Information, as a technique for sending messages, has three groups: Somatic, Media and Digital. Somatic information "... implies the effective presence, engagement, energy and sensitivity of the BODY for the production of signs" (p. 51). (LEVY, 1994) The author exemplifies this by citing the use of speech, dance, singing or instrumental music.

Media technologies, according to Lévy (1994), can be considered as molars, i.e. they "... fix and reproduce messages in order to ensure their greater reach and better diffusion in time and space" (p. 51). The examples cited by the author are traffic lights, paintings, jewelry and tapestries. It is transmitted to the media by means of reproductions of signs and marks, such as stamps, moldings, coins, etc. And writing, like drawing, is the "protomedia", i.e. a stage before the media. For Lévy (1994), the purpose of the media is to reproduce and transport messages. However, he points out that despite its great retroactive power, "... classic media is not, at first glance, a technique for engendering signs. It is content to fix, reproduce and transport a produced sound message" (LÉVY 1994, p. 52).

Based on Lévy (1994), Santiago (2010) states that information through sound language is more creative and interactive when compared to media in terms of the wealth of possibilities for sign interactions between communicators. For the digital message, the result of the New Information/Communication Technologies, it would still be above the media, because, "... it is the absolute of the montage, which affects the smallest fragments of the message, an indefinite and incessantly reopened availability for the combination, the mixing, the reordering of signs..." (LÉVY, 1994, p. 53).

For the development of this message, the main vehicle for this type of information is information technology and/or computer science. It is as creative and engenders signs as somatics itself. Computing is a molecular technique, says Lévy (1994). It is not merely a reproducer and disseminator of messages, like the media. It makes possible not only the interweaving of signs, but,

6

above all, modifications so subtle that they create and determine major reactions between the communicators and the object of their messages, in other words, "... the digital authorizes the manufacture of messages, their modification and even the interaction between them, atom of information by atom of information, bit by bit" (LÉVY, 1994, p. 53).

According to Santiago (2010), the development of the so-called New Information/Communication Technologies, with their digital dissemination, have provided mankind with a range of resource possibilities, from their use in the various fields of scientific knowledge construction, through to their application in all work activities and culminating, why not say it, in the entertainment industry itself.

"We are living through a frank and broad process of evolution of the technological-digital expression of virtual communication between social communicants." (p.07). This expression has characterized what some authors, including Ganàscia (1993) and Lévy (2002), have postulated as "Artificial Intelligence" (SANTIAGO, 2010).

Artificial Intelligence is part of contemporary human life, taking into account its own improvement and with different applications, as a technological artifact of culture. Ganàscia (1993) states that "... most human skills can thus be formulated in logical terms and simulated on a computer" (p. 22).

"This has been a reality in our daily lives, that is, we are always resorting, in some way, to an artificial digital resource that performs tasks that range from the extreme of banality to the extreme of sophistication and competence to meet our needs" (SANTIAGO, 2010, p. 07).

Ganàscia (1993) considers Artificial Intelligence to be the "... science of machines..." (p. 25), which has as its technological essence "... a juxtaposition of application domains..." (p. 25), which, according to the author, presents a set of territories and possibilities to be conquered by Man. Even more specifically, the author says that "... artificial intelligence is a subterfuge, an artifice designed to dominate machines by giving them intelligence" (GANASCIA, 1993, p. 27).

It is no longer a simple product of human technological capacity, but rather a process that has been advancing over time until it reached its current "high-tech" dimension, which has come to have an impact on society as a whole (SANTIAGO, 2010 p. 08).

Ganàscia (1993) illustrates the advent of so-called Artificial Intelligence in our daily lives by pointing to "Pascal's machine (1623-1662)" as the first realization of this process, which aimed, in a simple and mechanical way, to perform mathematical operations of addition and subtraction. According to Ganàscia (1993), Leibniz (1716-1846) presented us with a model of a machine capable of "... reasoning..." (p. 28), that is, in the author's view, a machine "... capable of stringing together elementary propositions to make deductions" (p. 28). Ganàscia (1993) goes on to offer

7

other examples until he considers the evolution of Artificial Intelligence to have taken place in the 20th century. He emphasizes that a fundamental historical milestone was identified at the meeting between electronic engineers, psychologists, cyberneticians and economists at Darmouth College, during a summer course, when John Mac Carthy "... proposed the creation of a new discipline that would be called artificial intelligence and that would aim to reproduce intelligent behaviour with the help of a machine" (GANASCIA, 1993, p. 44).

The use of information technology as a branch of Computer Science has undergone an inexhaustible process of improvement, resulting in a huge range of uses and appropriations in our own lives. From the capacity for the aesthetic creation of musical notes, to the fantastic discoveries of new mathematical theorems, from the formulation of new business management models to sophisticated surgical techniques, there are many strands and horizons of employability in and with computers. The very concept of how contemporary states operate requires their political and public agents to be restructured and trained in computerized networks.

In this regard, Lévy (2002) states that:

Relationships between people, work and intelligence itself all depend on the incessant metamorphosis of information devices of all kinds. Writing, reading, seeing, hearing, creating and learning are all captured by increasingly advanced information technology. For the author, scientific research can no longer be conceived of without a complex apparatus that redistributes the old divisions between experience and practice. At the end of the 20th century, a kind of knowledge by simulation is emerging that epistemologists have yet to invent (LÉVY, 2002, p. 7).

Reis and Col. (2008) state that the use of new methods to improve the nursing service, together with the considerable amount of information both in terms of care and the administration of hospital nursing, has corroborated the use of computer technology.

The computer revolution has contributed to the expansion of mental capacity. We can see that technological advances have created changes in various areas of modern life, since all organizations use some form of technology to carry out their operations and perform their tasks (REES, 1978).

In the area of health, specifically, biomedical and information technology have significantly influenced the ability to address the biggest problems facing health care today (LOPES and COL., 2011).

Computerization as a way of managing, administering, organizing, classifying, monitoring and obtaining relevant information in real time has made access to nursing indicators dynamic and productive (SCHOUT and NOVAES, 2007).

According to Santos (2013), the impression of the use of information technology in the health sector is that it is ten to fifteen years behind other sectors such as banking, industry and aviation. As a result, as a field of study, nursing is at a disadvantage when it comes to the use of information systems, automation and technological equipment (SANTOS, 2013).

The author reports that given this reality, it is important to consider that nursing practice can reach levels of excellence through the use of information systems. These systems should be an integral part of nursing care as a support tool for obtaining data and generating new information and knowledge (SANTOS, 2013).

Lopes and Col. (2011) point out that in nursing, new and complex challenges are being faced regarding the implementation and use, evaluation and development of these new technologies. Current nursing is supported and improved by the new knowledge that comes from technology, but there is no change in the basic essence of nursing practice (LOPES and COL., 2011).

Évora (2005) points out that the field of nursing informatics is gaining momentum, since it is an era in which information is the opening concerning the benefits it brings.

This points to the need for health professionals to be aware of the impacts of this new technological evolution on society, and consequently, the achievement of nursing professionals, in the face of the use of technology, in order to benefit the patient, reduce costs and rationalize work. (VIDAL et al., 2002)

^ Computer in Nursing

Based on the above propositions by Santiago (2010), Ganàscia (1993) and Lévy (2002). We reflect that the correlation between Nursing and the Computer is a social practice of work outlined by a combination of knowledge that is fed back by scientific-technological assumptions.

Évora (1998) states that information technology brings benefits to clients because it allows nurses to become more available for care, freeing them from the bureaucratic nursing process that ends up distancing them from care. From the author's perspective, the use of computers for information planning involves four assumptions: 1-"... the speed with which information can be obtained; 2- easy access to information; 3- the availability of new information and; 4- the convenience of the information" (ÉVORA, 1998 p. 17). The author emphasizes that this is possible through the concept of Nursing Information Systems. Based on Saba & McCornick, Évora (1998) says that these systems "... use the computer to process data into information and support the types of nursing activities or functions" (p. 17).

The author also draws a parallel line of reasoning based on a chronological presentation of the evolution of the use of computers in the health sector, particularly in hospitals, highlighting their introduction in the 1960s in the USA. She also recalls that computers were large, "... used basically

9

for the development of administrative functions such as: billing, payment, accounting and tax statistics" (ÉVORA, 1998 p. 24). In this period, according to the author, their use by nurses was very little observed.

These statements are corroborated by Évora, Hannah and Col. (2009) who mention that: "... The nursing profession recognizes the potential of information technology to improve practice and the quality of patient care. New roles are emerging for nurses: 1- Informatics as a specialty in nursing (recognized by the ANA - (American Nurses Association) in 2001; 2- Hospitals and other organizations are hiring nursing informatics specialists and consultants to help design and implement information systems; 3- Nurse educators use information systems to manage teaching environments; 4- Computerized information systems are used to teach, evaluate and identify specific student problem areas, as well as to obtain data on how students learn, process data for research and provide resources for continuing education; 5-The use of computerized systems by nurse researchers" (HANNAH and COL., 2009, p.21).

Évora (1998) goes on to say that, at the end of the 1960s and the beginning of the 1970s, the improvement and mastery of computer technology made it possible to use computers personally, including by reducing their size. Évora (1998) says that this greatly facilitated the expansion of the use of information systems within hospitals, with repercussions in the clinical area, communicating and storing data on clients. As a result, nurses began to recognize the importance of computers in their daily work, substantially improving their practice.

However, the author points out that there was a lot of resistance to the use of computers in nursing, pointing to studies that mention little acceptance of the advantages provided by the use of computers in nursing at the time. Évora (1998) deduced that this resistance was most probably due to a set of consequences, sustained mainly by "... inadequate experience and lack of knowledge and exposure to the computer" (p. 24).

A study carried out in the 1970s by the INTERNATIONAL FEDERATION FOR INFORMATION PROCESSING, addressed by Anderson in 1992, where some considerations highlighted the need for nurses to acquire knowledge about the use and exploitation of information technology.

In analyzing this issue during the 1980s, Évora (1998) found that it was fundamental, there was an increase in the development of integrated hospital information systems, through "... modules aimed at nursing activities" (p. 25).

Particularly in the USA, the concept of Nursing Information Systems was introduced, according to Évora (1998) citing Kiley et al. The author points out that, even though the first experiences of computer use by Brazilian nursing took place around the mid-1980s, its use was still timid compared to other professionals. She also points out that currently some isolated advances have been made in hospital centers, in an attempt not to lose sight of humanized care, a threat that could fuel resistance and/or prejudice within nursing itself.

The use of New Technologies by Nursing, in its different fields, is addressed by Mendes et al. (2000) who reveal this theme from the perspective of Nursing Communication, highlighting that there is a trend and some challenges that nurses will face in the 21st century.

Mendes et al. (2000) reaffirm their prepositions by quoting:

"Growing technological innovations, the development of new means of social coexistence, instant or real-time communications, the speed of transportation, the continuous overcoming of the frontiers of scientific knowledge, the consolidation of the third sector, are changes that, in Srouer's words, are sensitively redesigning social spaces" (MENDES and COL., p. 217).

Mendes et al. (2000), state that "... with the technology already available, investment in infrastructure and shared tools will lead not only to a considerable reduction in costs, but also to better care for all patients" (p. 220). In the authors' view, however, these innovations will bring with them some important implications that need to be considered, even before choosing them as the essence of nursing care. Under no circumstances should technology be seen as a substitute for the professional, but rather as a valuable tool to help plan specific and general nursing actions, according to the circumstances, contexts and singularities of each situation, each client, or even those that concern teaching, research and management activities.

On the possible effects of the benefits derived from the mastery, incorporation and application of information technology by nurses, Mendes et al. (2000) are affirmative in demarcating two groups exposed to the demand for the use of New Information/Communication Technologies: "? a) on the one hand, prepared patients, who demand more information and more investment in their own health and; b) on the other hand, internet-savvy health professionals who use new tools to offer more qualified care" (MENDES e COL., p. 220).

It is therefore vital for nursing to be prepared and trained to face this challenge, seeking, right from the undergraduate process, to insert a series of didactic-pedagogical strategies that move in this direction. The computer has already been definitively inserted into the world of contemporary work relations. Computer technology is becoming increasingly important for all of us. This is an irreversible process in which the alliance of technological knowledge and professional practices requires people who are ready to take on this challenge, including nurses.

With the advent of information technology, there are new possibilities for collective creation, cooperative learning and collaboration in networks, which has led to a questioning of the work

11

process in institutions, both companies and schools (LEVY, 1994).

Bastos and Guimaraes (2003) reinforce that computer-mediated teaching uses the *Internet* to store, retrieve and organize information, as well as to monitor students' progress and work, enabling greater flexibility, creativity, dynamism, interaction and communication in the educational process in the field of nursing.

Christiane et al. (2004) state that these technologies are driving distance learning and are a way of promoting continuing education for health professionals. Faced with accelerated technological development and the speed with which it becomes obsolete.

In nursing, informatics has been the subject of many national and international inquiries and studies that seek to identify and describe the skills related to the use of computers by nurses, define the content to be taught, and evaluate the disciplines of informatics in nursing. The fundamental purpose of this area refers to the use of computer technologies in nursing (PERES and COL., 2001).

The development of information technology has brought about the need to use computers in various human activities, including school activities. (PEREZ and COL., 2007)

Computers help to improve education and the quality of teachers and administrators in health care institutions (VIDAL and COL., 2002).

The incorporation of new technological resources into the education of professionals has become a major challenge for Brazilian nursing, and these resources have been little explored by nursing schools (MARQUES and MARIN, 2004).

Thus, Marin (1998) advocates the creation of a Nursing Informatics Discipline aimed at developing competencies and skills in nursing informatics in order to understand the application of its resources in professional practice and not just to be instructed in basic computer skills.

Luis et al. (1995) defend the idea that in order to have an understanding of the use of computer resources in nursing practice, it is necessary for computer teaching to promote interdisciplinarity by defining a network of relationships between the various disciplines of the degree, thus not being carried out in an isolated discipline.

Therefore, the subject of nursing informatics should not only focus on basic training in informatics itself (text editors, presentations, *chats*, forums, etc.), but should allow students to visualize the potential and limitations of using these resources in their professional practice (PERES and COL., 2007).

The above authors conclude that computer-mediated teaching in nursing is a challenge to be overcome, requiring changes in the attitude of students and teachers towards the educational process.

^ Health Education and Educational Technologies

Technological innovation and computers are constantly changing the activities of modern society (FONSECA et al 2009).

Computer systems used for teaching are known as CAI (Computer Assisted Instruction). The main objective of these systems is to transmit information on a given subject (ZEM-MASCARENHAS; CASSIAN, 2001).

Health education relies on countless technological resources and, in line with developments in telecommunications, health professionals and patients can now access a wealth of information quickly. This means of access provides nurses with the opportunity to address issues relating to health promotion, disease prevention and the acquisition of information and nursing interventions (HANNAH et al 2009).

In the first decades of the 20th century, specialized technologies and innovations emerged in the area of computerization, facilitating the dissemination of information (CECAGNO; SIQUEIRA; CEZAR VAZ, 2005). Technological changes and developments in research have become outdated, as we live in a world of rapid and constant innovation (ZEM-MASCARENHAS, 2002; ZEM-MASCARENHAS; CASSIANI, 2001). Computer-assisted instruction can help users enrich their ability to exchange information with computers, preparing them for their future role in a technological society.

In a study by Nietsche, educational technology is defined as: A body of knowledge enriched by the action of man and is not just about the construction and use of artifacts or equipment. The technological process involves knowing how to use knowledge and equipment in all everyday situations, whether critical, routine or not. (PERES, et al, 2001).

This concept demonstrates that technology applied to education should be possible from the planning stage to the monitoring of the educational system, with a view to making a systematic set of knowledge possible. Information technology in nursing has become an indispensable accessory, not just using the computer as a place to store data, but using it as a facilitator in the teaching-learning process for both the professionals and the clients involved in this process (PERES, et al, 2001).

The audiovisual resource can provide a better understanding of the information offered and can also be used to help reduce the time spent by the person using it. (PAULA& CARVALHO, 1997, p36).

In this way, the use of an audiovisual resource can be an important strategy for orienting and educating patients.

A qualitative change in the teaching/learning process occurs when it is possible to integrate technologies such as telematics, audiovisual, textual, oral, musical, playful and bodily. Video explores seeing and visualizing. It develops vision with multiple slices of reality through visual rhythms with images situated in the present, interconnected with the past and the future. Seeing is related to speaking, narrating or telling stories. Spoken narration anchors the process of meaning (MORAN, 2000).

This reminds us of the importance of this resource in health information. It is assumed that the development of new instructional programs allied to educational technology, used by educators and students can collaborate in the use of these resources, taking advantage of the advantages offered for better nursing teaching as well as for health education.

^ Use of the Central Venous Catheter

The first experiments to catheterize a central vein began in 1929, when Forssmann inserted a sterile tube into a vein in his arm and described the advantages of this method. In 1952, Aubaniac performed the first venous catheterization of the subclavian vein and several other procedures followed, such as the advent of parenteral nutrition. The use of central venous catheterization has increased considerably since 1968, making this a clinical procedure with improved therapeutic options (BASILE, FILHO, 1998). This practice has greatly assisted the work of nurses.

In 1983, the Totally Implanted Central Venous Catheter (TI CVC) began to be marketed, allowing access to the central vascular system without a catheter on the outside of the skin. This type of catheter was initially aimed exclusively at patients undergoing cancer treatment who required frequent and intermittent venous access (PHILLIPS, 2001). Currently, the indication for this catheter is still exclusive to patients undergoing chemotherapy.

Fully implanted venous catheters do not have any externalized parts after installation.

The device consists of two main parts: the access body, whose chamber can be made of stainless steel or titanium, with a central part that is covered by a sealing silicone diaphragm, which can receive from one thousand to two thousand punctures, has a diameter of 2 to 3 cm, and the second part is the radiopaque catheter made of silicone, polyurethane or Teflon (PHILLIPS, 2001).There is currently a range of devices and different materials on the market.

To activate the catheter, you need a specific needle with an appropriate *bevel* that allows penetration and removal without damaging the diaphragm. The appropriate needle is the *Huber* or *Cytocan* type, which are available in various sizes (INCA, 2008). Using a needle that does not meet these standards can damage the catheter.

14

Because it is a type of catheter with an indefinite lifespan, it is indicated for treatment with chemotherapy drugs and can be used for infusion of other drugs (PERCIVAL, SL, 2005). The patient's lack of clinical conditions, such as thrombocytopenia, low *(PS) Performance Status* and impairment of one or more noble organs, are factors that indicate against implantation, as a small surgical procedure is required to implant it and maintenance and manipulation requires the use of a needle, which increases the risk of bleeding and even the development of venous thrombosis. The same applies to the prevention of infection by bacteria and fungi.

III - THEORETICAL-METHODOLOGICAL FOUNDATION

^ **The study design**

The method: this was a qualitative observational study in which 20 (twenty) nursing consultations for patients before starting chemotherapy were monitored.

The type of study: Intervention research, with qualitative analysis under the reference of Bardin, J. (2002), for content analysis, with the final result being a multimedia technological production, characterized by the development of a multimedia educational resource for guidance on what a long-term venous catheter is like.

Intervention research aimed at finding an immediate solution to an existing problem. Changing a problematic situation through systematic planning is the ultimate goal of this type of research, which in this case is to be able to answer the patient's questions and provide guidance on the use of a permanent venous catheter to ensure venous access for chemotherapy treatment (POLIT; BECK; HUNGLER, 2004).

Research related to the development of products and processes according to the needs or solutions to problems of interest to society (APPOLINARIO, F, 2006; GONÇALVES, 2010).

Data Collection Techniques:

During the period from April to May 2014, 20 nursing consultations were monitored in an exclusive chemotherapy outpatient clinic. The consultations were with patients who needed to have a central venous catheter inserted in order to start chemotherapy treatment, observing the information resources used by the nursing professional to convey the messages, and the questions openly asked by the patient at the time of the information received.

Direct observation - a field diary was used (Appendix -1), which showed which resources nurses use to inform patients that they need to place a central venous catheter.

Open-ended interviews - based on an analysis of the speeches of patients who agreed to take part in the study and signed an informed consent form for questions and doubts, who were interviewed through open-ended questions (Appendix 2) about their main doubts about the catheter.

^**Data processing:** Analysis constructed using the discourse analysis modality. The open questions, shown in Table I, were classified by analogy of the speeches and the consequent construction of the nuclear categories/ideas that emerged from the process of categorizing the field observations and the patients' speeches.

According to Bardin's definition (1988),

16

"Content analysis is a set of techniques for analyzing communications. It is not an instrument, but a range of tools; or more strictly speaking, it will be a single instrument, but marked by a great variety of forms and adaptable to a very wide field of application: communications" (p. 31).

In this Content Analysis, the information from the speeches and discourses of previously investigated subjects about doubts about the catheter was treated in such a way that the nucleus of related ideas that point to a categorization of themes. Bardin (1988) refers to categorization:

"Categorization is an operation of classifying the constituent elements of a set, by differentiating them and then regrouping them according to genre (analogy), using previously defined criteria. Categories are headings or classes, which bring together a group of elements (recording units, in the case of content analysis) under a generic heading, a grouping made on the basis of the characteristics of these elements...".

(p. 117).

According to Bardin (1988), content analysis aims to understand what is contained in the discourse, in other words, the meaning of the subjects' speech. That which is "implied" and/or hidden in the discourse, seeking to decode it into units of understanding and subsequent categories and nuclei of thematic ideas.

Bardin (1988) highlights three important stages that the researcher must respect in the process of establishing categories and their possible analysis:

1 - Pre-Analysis; 2 - Exploration of the material and; 3 - Treatment and interpretation of the results. Following the referenced stages:

In the first stage, the source material was thoroughly analyzed. The entire content of the field diary and the questions posed by the patients.

They then extracted the content, keeping it consistent with the subject matter and the categories represented. There was no rigor in the evaluation of the source, because what was wanted was familiarization with the possible details attached to the speeches and/or documents. The steps followed.

1.   Rule of Exhaustiveness, i.e. the search for all the elements of the source analyzed;

2.   Rule of Representativeness, i.e. a significant sample to obtain the selected speeches from the researched source;

3.   Rule of homogeneity, which should be the common characteristics present in the source, the same theme and;

4.   The rule of relevance is that the source must be closely related to the subject being

researched.

These four basic rules outlined by Bardin (1988) formed the basis for the entire Pre-Analysis stage of the questionnaires applied to the subjects. With regard to the second stage illustrated by Bardin (1988), about the exploration of the speeches, it took place through structuring by means of two strategies called: inventory of the units of records and context (meaning) and; classification by analogy, that is, the separation of these units of records and context, in order to achieve the organization of the messages, for later analysis and discussion. According to Bardin (1988), in the inventory of units, the elements of the discourse are isolated and, in the classification by analogy, the elements are broken down, imposing an organization on the messages.

As for the third and final stage, the treatment and interpretation of the results, the units arising from the speeches were grouped, thanks to the creation of tables/inventories indicating these units, which allowed us to highlight the thematic categories, with their own nuclei.

After this survey, the data was analyzed qualitatively using Bardan's framework and, after categorization, a script was created for the development of a multimedia with marketing professionals to meet the expectations pointed out by patients about the catheter, to be presented in the nursing consultation, facilitating the nurse's approach to the subject of central venous catheters.

Ethical issues: Patients who attended a nursing consultation at a chemotherapy outpatient clinic in a private institution in Rio de Janeiro participated in this study, with the inclusion criterion of being indicated for placement of a fully implanted central venous catheter. After being informed of the aim of the study, they agreed to take part by signing an informed consent form (Appendix -3).

This research began after approval by the Research Ethics Committee of the Federal University of the State of Rio de Janeiro (UNIRIO), according to the attached report.

IV- RESULTS

Pre-analysis:

Exhaustive reading of the field diary and patient discourse (taken from the Open Interviews), identifying the core words and common questions asked by the patients.

Field diary analysis:

The field diary showed the informative methodology used by the nurses to pass on the message.

The informative techniques presented by the nurses to indicate the placement of the catheter were based on identifying the treatment proposed for the patient, quantifying the amount of infusion and the chemical characteristics of the drugs to be infused and the patient's venous access conditions.

The nurses had a simulator model of the catheter, a visual resource of the material used for the procedure and the catheter itself. After the practical demonstration of the model, the patients asked questions.

The doubts and questions raised were recorded in order to draw up the script.

- **Total consultations** 20

- **Didactic material used by the nurse;** Catheter and demonstration dummy.

- **Specialist Nurses Observed:** 03 are the nurses who carry out nursing consultations at the institution.

Nurses' speeches:

The nurses followed a pattern to assess the patient and present the proposal to place the catheter:

"The catheter is a device, (visual practical demonstration with model and device), which is in the vein and the puncture part is under the skin, a proper needle (practical demonstration) enters the puncture chamber of the catheter which is made of silicone, the whole procedure is sterile. The nurse separates all the sterile material and puts on a mask and cap before puncturing the catheter."

Table I - Inventory of patient questions. 2015

Inventory of Patient Doubts	fi	%
Does the catheter enter the vein?	18	90
Does the catheter stay in the vein?	16	80
Can you clog the vein?	5	20

What material is the catheter made of?	2	10
The catheter goes straight into the vein	14	70
Does it hurt to put the catheter in?	18	90
Does it hurt to put the needle in the catheter?	10	50
How thin or thick is the needle?	8	40
Do I have to go under anesthesia?	8	40
What kind of anesthesia?	8	40
Do you have to be hospitalized?	14	70
Can you get wet in the shower?	18	90
Does it move at all?	10	50
How is the dressing?	8	40
If I go to a hospital, can they use it?	8	40
What's it like to sleep?	8	40
I can lead a normal life	8	40
Is anything left out?	8	40
TOTAL NUMBER OF QUESTIONS	200	100

There was a high frequency and repetition of doubts when asked about the catheter.

Table II - Categorization of the inventory of patients' doubts 2015

Categories	Sub-categories	Thematic Units	fi	%
What is a catheter?	Presentation of the material	The catheter	39	19
Where is the catheter?	In the vein, stopped, clogged/	The location	22	11
Is it painful?	Does it hurt to put it in?	Pain	66	33
What are the precautions? What about the bath?	What do I need to do at home? Care		74	37

And to sleep?

Total questions	*200*	100

After determining the frequency of questions by category, a group of 3 nurses specialized in oncology nursing was assembled to prepare the answers. The answers were taken from the referenced scientific literature.

Table III Answers to the questions and theoretical framework. 2015

Thematic Units	Answers	Reference
The catheter and its location	During chemotherapy, the veins progressively lose their ability to receive drugs and become more difficult to puncture. The doctor in charge may suggest implanting the fully implantable catheter. A safe device that facilitates venous infusion by making it easier for the drug to enter the vein.	NS302 Ingran P Lavery I (2005) Peripheral intravenous therapy: key risks and implications for practice. Nursing Standboard 19, 46, 5564
Pain	It doesn't hurt to put the catheter in because there is anesthesia. The decision on the type of anesthesia is made between the surgeon and the patient, and there is no need for hospitalization. It hurts to puncture, but it's just a little prick with a catheter needle.	www.venousdigest.com
Care	As it is inserted internally, the device is not visible, there is only a small protrusion, so there is no need for bandages, which means that the patient doesn't have to be so careful when it comes to moving around. If it's not in use, you can bathe and sleep normally. The procedure is carried out by a trained professional using sterile material and a needle suitable for access. Monthly	Up to date.com

maintenance is required outside of treatment.

The answers were objective and categorized according to thematic unit.

■ Roadmap

The results were sent to specialized media professionals who prepared the following script for the video. **Job:** fully implantable venous catheter (Port-a-Cath®)**Date:** July 29, 2014 to 6'

Time	Audio	Video
1'	Researched trail	Animation: Fully implantable venous catheter
	Loc masc OFF : During chemotherapy, the veins progressively lose their ability to receive drugs and become more difficult to puncture.	Passing effect
	Loc masc OFF : Faced with this scenario, the doctor in charge may suggest implanting the catheter completely	Animated lettering: Peripheral veins
	implantable. This device is extremely safe and facilitates venous infusion.	Animated lettering: Deployment
	Loc masc OFF : Inserting the catheter	Scenario: Hospital - care area
	takes place under local anesthesia, in a small surgery that takes between 30 minutes and an hour. In this procedure	Dialogue takes place between patient and
	surgically, the device is inserted under the skin in the thoracic region, making it very small.	the Nurse
	visible.	Passing effect
	Patient: Does it hurt to put the catheter in?	Passing effect
	Nurse: It doesn't hurt to put the catheter in because there's anesthesia.	
	Animation: Fully implantable venous catheter	Scenario: Hospital - care area
	Animated lettering *effect*: Veins	
	peripheral	Dialogue takes place between patient and nurse
2'	Animated lettering: Deployment	Animated lettering: General information
	Scenario: Hospital - area	
	Assistance	Scenario: Hospital - care area
	(E) After placement, the medication goes through the catheter straight into the vein.	Dialogue takes place between patient and nurse
	(E) The decision on the type of anesthesia is between the surgeon and the patient and there is no need for hospitalization.	Animated lettering: Comfort and mobility
		Illustrations
	(Q) Does it hurt to put the needle in?	Illustrations

22

	(E) It hurts, but it's just a little prick with a catheter needle.	Illustrations
2'	*(Q)* If I go to a hospital, can they use my catheter? *(E)* If there are trained professionals and own needle, yes.	
	(E) Because it is inserted internally, the.	Passing effect
	The device is not visible, there is only a small protrusion, which eliminates the need for bandages and does not require the patient to take as much care when moving.	Illustrations Splash: Technical talk
1	*(Q)* Can I lead a normal life? *(E)* Yes, it's quite possible. If the punctured needle is missing, nothing will show.	Passing effect

05/08/2014 - The group of specialists in oncology nursing met to read and correct the script, when they changed the sequence of the presentation and added technical information about the catheter and maintenance periods at the end of the script.

The design and animation support team met the requests and then produced the story board, which would be the media preview.

^ Story Board

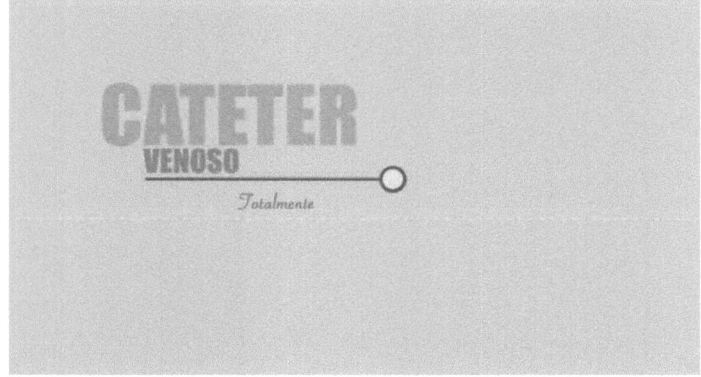

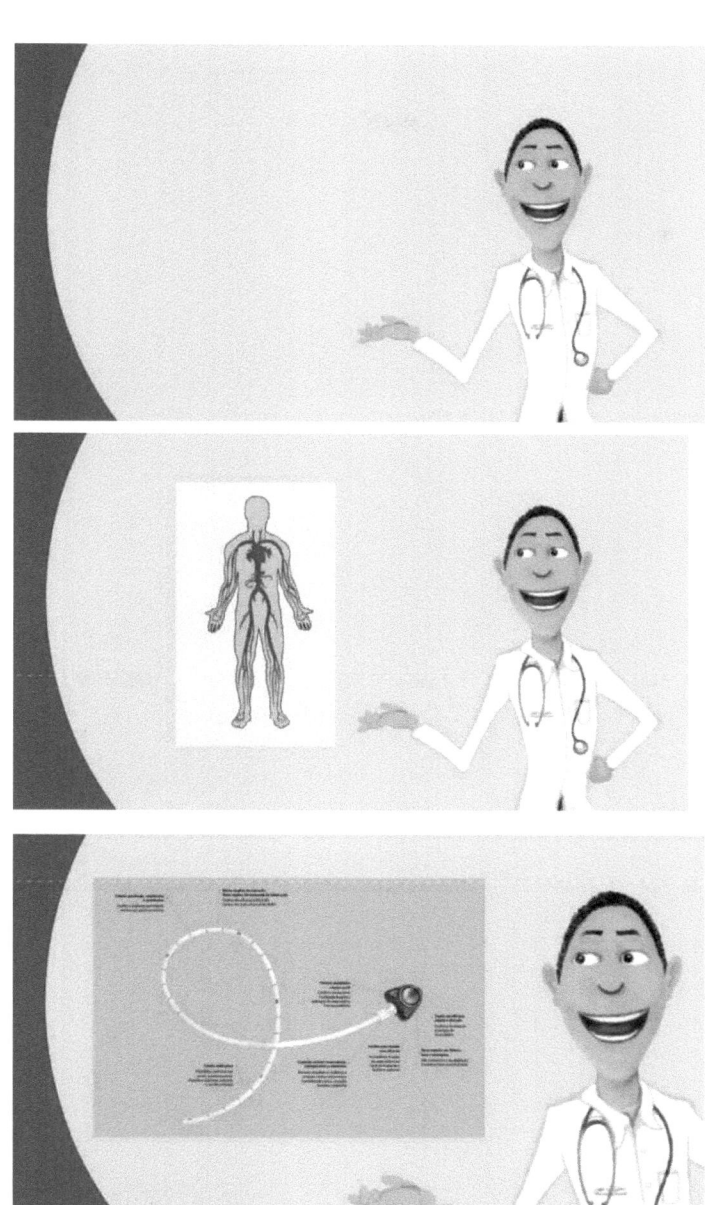

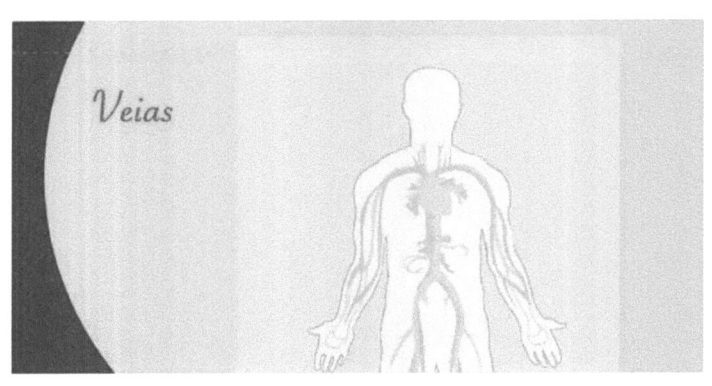

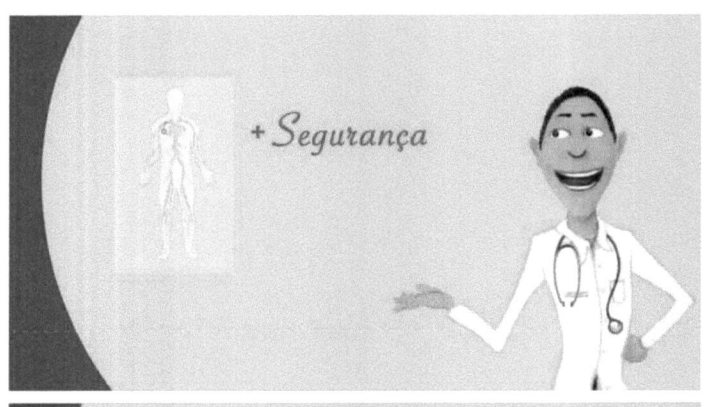

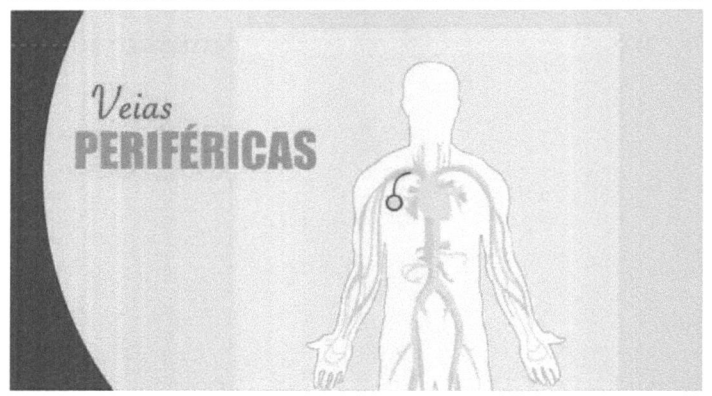

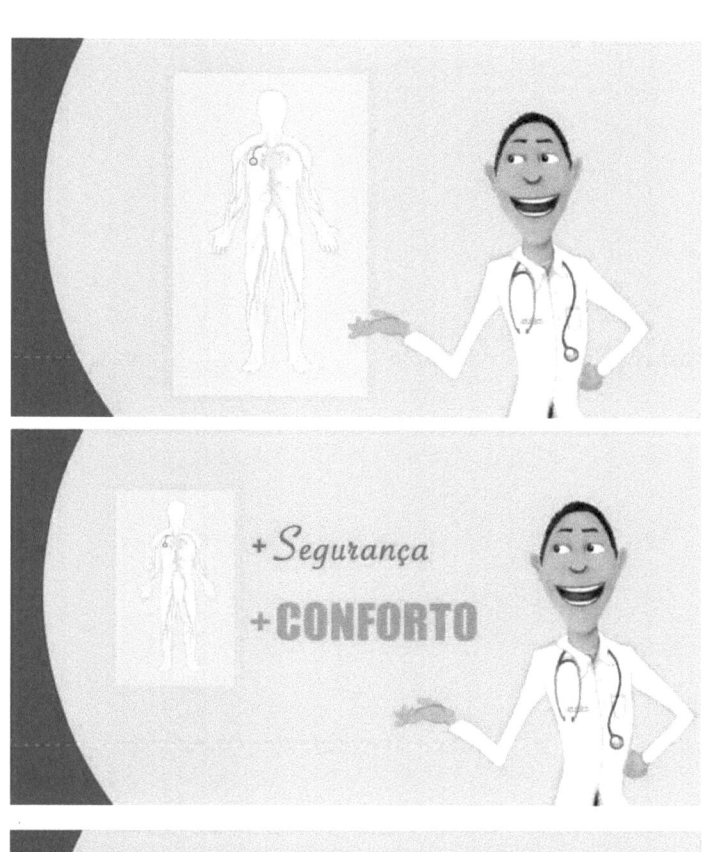

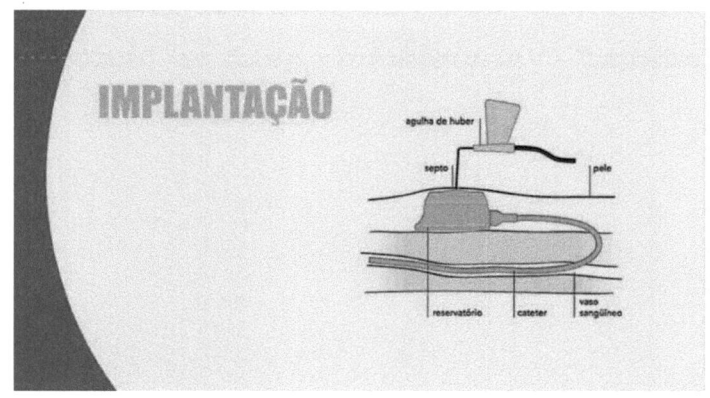

ANESTESIA

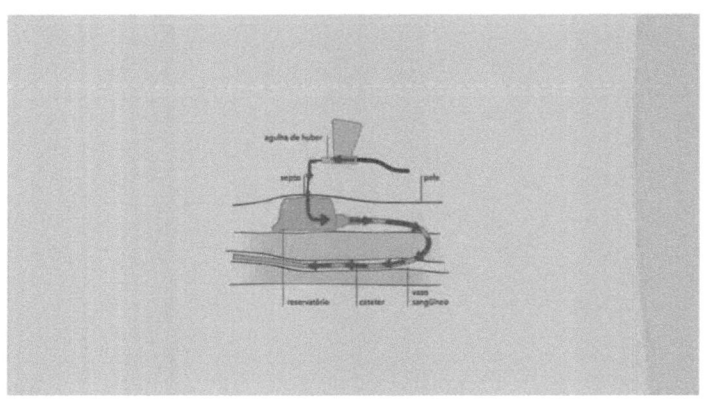

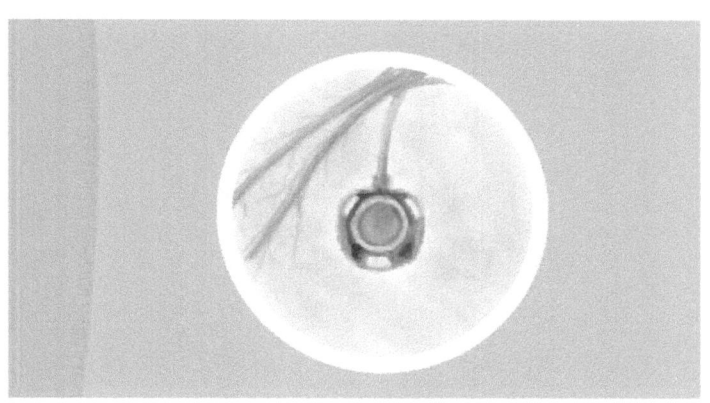

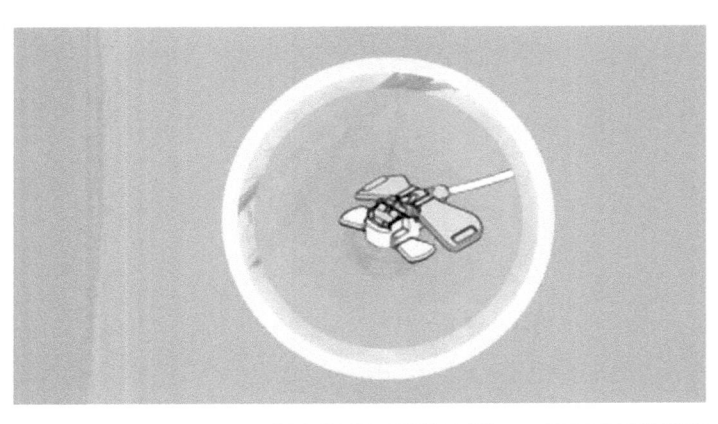

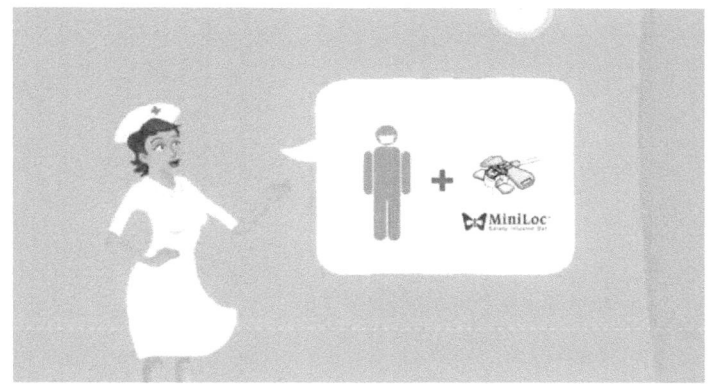

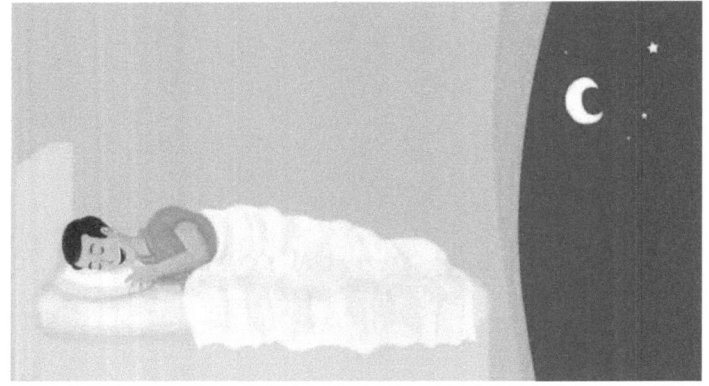

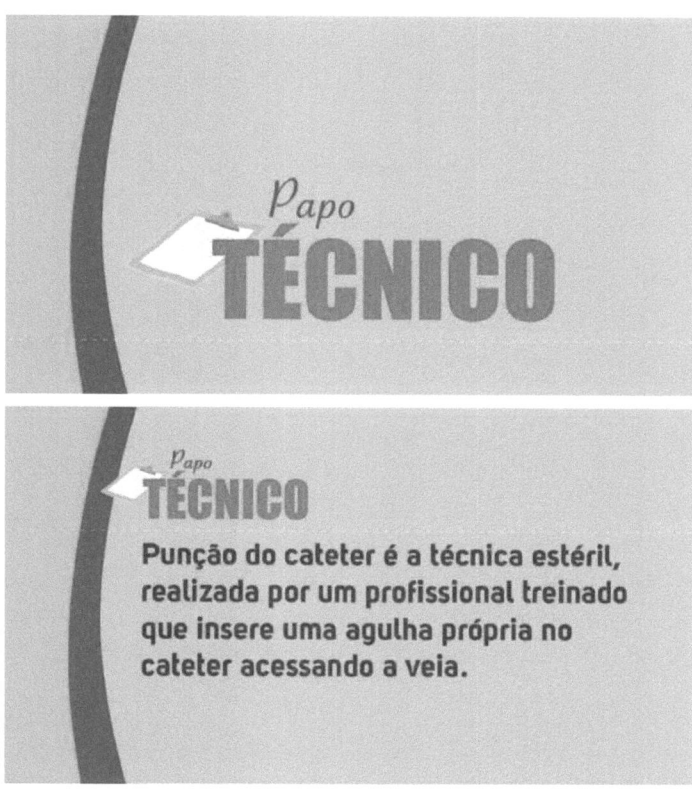

Story board analysis,

The Board presented was analyzed by a group of specialists in oncology nursing and marketing professionals when they defined the visual and brand identity, opting for the removal of pink colors and keeping the nude and blue tones, requesting the removal of the imprint of the needle mark in the animation. Better definition of the catheter and bed designs was requested.

^ **The program used to create the media.**

To create the media, the *Addobe Suite* program was used, which allows for the creation and movement of drawings.

Multi-professional team that completed the work:

Soundtrack _ Motion Blurfix Company;

Drawing _ Prepared by Thonny Willian de Mello

Animation _ Producers Thonny Willian de Mello and Silvei Corrêia, both from Motion Blurfix.

Script _ Alline Menegueti, BMR Medical

The requested changes were made and the film was produced, which can currently be viewed at the following address

- https://www.youtube.com/watch?v=OV_1STIQ6PCw

- https://drive.google.com/drive/u/0/#folders/0BzEnYclPucjoSGp5R3NfMXhpNUO

V - CONCLUSION

According to CRESPO ET al, (2015), several innovative, comprehensive and universally accessible multimedia products have been developed by nurses in the last five years: software, blogs, wiki, webquest, videos and CD-ROOMs, e-books. A variety of tools to help and improve the care provided by nursing professionals to guide the health of their patients. The authors also point out that in order to develop and create these works, it was necessary to include various professionals, from the fields of communication and health, as well as information technologists. They also had to follow research protocols, not only to identify the need and demand, but also to prepare the final product. This was clearly seen in the creation of this multimedia for answers to questions about catheters.

The core of this multimedia is made up of information and a visual support, the latter being what makes the message visible. The communication support is visual, made up of structure, shape, module, texture, color and movement, which are transcribed into encrypted messages.

It should be noted that non-verbal reading plays a part in the material, as one of the mechanisms for producing meaning, integrated with other fields of knowledge, acting on the individual's general culture. It represents a link between communication and knowledge, that is, between what is seen and what is retained, between what is retained and what is expressed, between what is expressed and what is expected to be seen, guaranteeing greater understanding of the message.

The informative multimedia based on questions from patients guarantees the development of resources that are objective to the understanding of a given group, which makes the video different in its content when compared to commercial media produced by industries that want to sell their product.

The material produced here seeks to answer the simple questions of a user of a particular product, and meets the needs of health professionals who use the product as a facilitator of information identified by the needs of a group of users.

The detailed script, based on legitimate research, will be an example of the undeniable care that should be applied to information products intended for any kind of health advice.

During the study, a number of information resources were found to have been produced without legitimate research criteria, which does not guarantee the source of the information.

It is believed after the work has been done that there is a need for guarantees that products with health information and care guidelines are rigorously analyzed and the result of scientific research before they are exposed to users, and that there is also a need to test such products.

It is possible to assume that the Carefully material developed here will facilitate the patient's understanding and the nurse's educational work. However, there is a need to continue the study and validate the product developed and the result of its practical application to the daily lives of nurses and their patients in chemotherapy outpatient clinics.

However, in order to guarantee the quality of all health nursing information and guidance, to be used in freely accessible electronic media, we propose the creation of an information guarantee committee or seal based on scientific evidence.

REFERENCES

APPOLINARIO, F. Metodologia da ciência: filosofia e pràtica da pesquisa. ... Blumenau: Diretiva, 2006.

ASSAD, A.L. D; SOUZA, R.F.de. Challenges of innovation in the area of continuous debate, Cadernos de História da Ciência- Instituto Butanta- Vol. V, jul-dez2009.

BASTOS, M.A.R., Guimaraes E.M.P. Distance education in nursing: report of an experience. Rev. Lat. Am Enferm. 2003; 11(5): 685-91.

BARDIN, L. Content Analysis. Translated by Luiz Antero Reto Augusto Pinheiro, Lisbon: Setenta 1988.

BASILE-FILHO, A.; OLIVEIRA E CASTRO, P.T.; JÙNIOR, G.A.P.; MARSON, F.; JÙNIOR, L.M.; COSTA, J.T. Primary sepsis related to central vascular catheters,

Intensive Care Medicine Symposium: Infection and Shock; Ribeirao Preto Medical School, chapter III, v. 31, p. 363-368, 1998

BRUZI, LM; MENDES, DC, Importance of nursing care in the management of complications related to fully implantable catheters. Rev Esc Enferm USP; 45(2): 5226 2011

CECAGNO, D. SIQUEIRA, H.C.H. CESAR VAZ, M.R., Talking about research, education and health in nursing   ,   2010,   Available   at:
http://www.litoral.ufpr.br/sites/default/files/Revista Etc%26Tae n01.pdf

CRESPO, A. SCAVARDA, A. PASSOS, P.ELICHER, M.J.SANTIAGO, LC. , Management in health multimedia/Nursing productions, BMR, spetial issue,v.5 n.5 Jan,2015. Available at: http://www.businessjournalz.org/bmr/

ÉVORA, Y. D. M. O Paradigma da Informàtica em Enfermagem. Associate Professor Thesis presented to the Ribeirao Preto Nursing School of the University of Sao Paulo, 1998.

. Informatics in Nursing Care £ IN: Carmem Elizabeth Kalinowski (Org.) Programa de Atualizaçao em Enfermagem: saùde do adulto. PROENF. Porto Alegre: Artmed, 2006, p. 43-92.

. Process of computerization in nursing: basic guidelines. Sao Paulo: EPU; 2005.

FERREIRA, A.K.S.L. CAPONERO, F., TEIXEIRA M.J., Pain induced by antineoplastic chemotherapy, mechanism of prevention and treatment Pràtica Hospitalar Sao Paulo, n57, p14450, Mai-Jun 2008).

FIGUEIREDO,M.F.S; RODRIGUES_NETO,JF:LEITE: M.T.S. Modelos aplicados às atividades em educaçao em saùde Rev Bras Enf , Brasilia. v 63 n 1 feb 210 Available at: http://www.scielo.br/pdf/reben/v63n1/v63n1a19.pdf on June 17, 2013

BARRA, DCC. NASCIMENTO, ERP do; MARTINS, J de J; ALBUQUERQUE, GL; ERDMAN, AL; Historical evolution and impact of technology in the area of health and nursing, Revista Eletrônica de Enfermagem, v. 08, n. 03, p. 422 - 430, 2006 Available at http://www.fen.ufg.br/revista/revista8_3/v8n3a13.htm

FROEHNER JÙNIOR, I. Totally implantable central venous catheters for chemotherapy in 100 patients with malignant neoplasms.Universidade Federal de SantaCatarina   :   Florianópolis, 2005. Available at: <

http://www.bibliomed.ccs.ufsc.br/CC0416.pdf > Accessed on: 03 May 20113

GANASCIA, J.G. A Inteligência Artificial. Lisbon: Piaget Institute, 1993.

HANNAH, K. J.; BALL, M. J.; EDWARDS, M. J. A. Introduction to Nursing Informatics. 3 ed. Porto Alegre: Artmed, 2009.

NATIONAL CANCER INSTITUTE. Basis of treatment. In: Ministério da Saù, editor. Açoes de enfermagem para o controle do câncer. Rio de Janeiro; 2008.

3ed. P. 409-466

LÉVY, P. A Inteligência Coletiva £ por uma antropologia do ciberespaço. Sao Paulo: Loyola, 1994.

. As Tecnologias da Inteligência: o futuro do pensamento na era da informàtica.Sao Paulo: Editora 34, 2002.

LOPES, A.C.C.; FERREIRA, A.A.; FERNANDES, J.A.L.; MORITA, A.B.P.S.; POVEDA,V.B.; SOUZA, A.J.S.Construction and evaluation of educational software on indwelling urinary catheterization. Rev Esc Enferm USP 2011; 45(1):215-22

MARQUES, I.R.; MARIN, H.F. Enfermagem na WEB: O processo de criaçao e valididaçao de um WEB site sobre doença arterial coronariana. Rev Lat Am Enferm [periodical on the Internet]. 2002[cited 2004 Jul. 20];10(3):[about 10 p.]. Available at:

http://www.scielo.br/scielo.php?script=sci_arttext&pid=S0104116920020003000005&lng=pt &nrm=iso

MENDES, I. A C. et al. Communication and Nursing: trends and challenges for the next millennium. Revista de Enfermagem da Escola Anna Nery, Rio de Janeiro: v. 4, n 7, p. 217- 224, aug/2000.

MORAN, J.M. ^Innovative Teaching and Learning with Audiovisual and Telematics

Technologies^, IN: MORAN, J. M. et all. New Technologies and Pedagogical Mediation. Campinas: Papirus. 2000.

PAULA, A.A.D.; CARVALHO, E.C.C. Teaching perioperative care to patients: a comparative study of audiovisual (video) and oral resources. Rev.latino-am.enfermagem , Ribeirao Preto, v. 5, n. 3, p. 35-42, July 1997.

PERES H.H.C., DUARTE Y.A.O., MAEDA S.T., COLVERO L.A. Exploratory study on the use of computer resources by undergraduate nursing students. Ver Esc Enferm USP. 2001;35(1):88-94.

POLIT,D.F.,BECK,C.T,HUNGKER,B.P Fundamentals of nursing research 5ed, Porto Alegre. Artemed,2004

PHILLIPS, L. D. Manual of Intravenous Therapy. Porto Alegre: Artmed, 2001.

REVELES,A.G., TAKAHASHI,R.T, Health education for ostomized patients, a bibliometric study. Rev. esc. Enferm. USP Sao Paulo v41, n2, june, 2007.

REES, R.L. Internet: understanding computers. J Nurs Admin. 1978;8(3):70-3.

REIS, E.A.A.; DENSER, C.P.A.C.; MINATEL, V.F.; BORK, A.M.T. Definition of Nursing Care Indicators based on minimum data [Internet]. [cited 2008 Jun. 21]. Available from: http://www.sbis.org.br/cbis9/arquivos/730.doc

SANTIAGO, L. C. A Informatizaçao dos Serviços de Enfermagem: a busca de informações acerca do uso do computador no cotidiano da pràtica profissional hospitalar. Post-Doctorate in Nursing, University of Sao Paulo, 2010.

SANTOS, A.S. A educaçao em saù reflexao e aplicabilidade em atença primària em saù, Ministério da saù 2007, Available at   at:

http://portal.saude.gov.br/portal/arquivos/pdf/caderno_de_educacao_popular_e_saude.pdf on May 20, 2013.

SCHOUT, D.; NOVAES, H.M.D. From record to indicator: managing the production of care information in hospitals. Ciênc. Saùde Coletiva. 2007;12(4):935-44.

VIDAL, E.M.; MARIA, J.E.B.; SANTOS G.L.S. Educaçao, informàtica e professores. Fortaleza: Demócrito Rocha; 2002.

ZEM-MASCARENHAS, SH. Apenenf: a web environment to support nursing teaching. In: Anais do 9° CongressoBrasileiro de Informàtica em Saù; 2004 nov. 7-10; Ri-beirao Preto [event on the Internet]. Sao Paulo: UNIFESP;2004, Available at:

http://telemedicina.unifesp.br/pub/SBIS/CBIS2004/trabalhos/arquivos/247.pdf.

APPENDIX 1

FIELD DIARY

Data Collection Instrument for the research entitled **Multimedia as an educational resource about long-term central venous catheters for clients undergoing chemotherapy.**

Author: Adriana de Souza Crespo

Advisor: Prof. Dr. Luiz Carlos Santiago

FIELD DIARY

Day // Time : _____ Sector:

Nurse:

A) Description of verbal or non-verbal resources used by the nurse to argue with the patient about the need to place the fully implanted catheter?

APPENDIX 2

INTERVIEW SCRIPT

1) What questions do you have about the long-term central venous catheter?

APPENDIX 3- INFORMED CONSENT FORM

Title: Multimedia as an educational resource about long-term central venous catheters for clients undergoing chemotherapy.

STUDY OBJECTIVE: The aim of this project is to develop a multimedia as an educational resource about long-term central venous catheters for clients undergoing chemotherapy; to evaluate the content of the multimedia with specialist nurses who advise clients about long-term central venous catheters.

ALTERNATIVE FOR PARTICIPATING IN THE STUDY: You have the right not to participate in this study. We are collecting information to develop a protocol for evacuating critical patients in times of fire. If you do not want to take part in the study, this will not interfere with your professional/student life.

STUDY PROCEDURE: If you decide to take part in this study, you will participate by answering individual questions that will last approximately 10 minutes, and we will use your answers as part of the research object.

RISKS: You may be anxious about the questions you will be asked

BENEFITS: The answers to your questionnaire will help to develop a CD/DVD to answer the main questions about a catheter for treatment, but it will not necessarily be for your direct benefit. However, being part of this study will provide you with more information about the place and relevance of these writings for the institution in question.

CONFIDENTIALITY: As stated above, your name will not appear in the texts of the project, nor on any forms to be filled in by us. No publication based on this questionnaire will reveal the names of any research participants. Without your written consent, the researchers will not disclose any research data in which you are identified.

DISCLAIMERS: This research is being carried out at the Clinicas Oncológicas Integradas-COI. It is linked to the Federal University of the State of Rio de Janeiro - UNIRIO through the Postgraduate Program in Health and Technology in the Hospital Space, with Adriana de Souza Crespo as the main researcher, under the supervision of Prof. Dr. Luiz Carlos Santiago.

The researcher will be available to answer any questions you may have. If necessary, please contact Adriana de Souza Crespo on (21) 98259-2042, or the Research Ethics Committee, CEP-UNIRIO 26651214.3.3001.5533 on 2542-7771 or e-mail cep- unirio@unirio.br. You will have a copy of this consent form to keep with you. You will provide your name, address and contact telephone number only so that the study team can contact you in case of need.

Name: _____

Phone: _____

I have read this document, which has two pages (obverse and reverse), and I agree to take part in this study.

Signature:

Date: _____

I discussed the research proposal with this participant and, in my opinion, he/she understood his/her alternatives (including not taking part in the research, if he/she so wished) and gave his/her free consent to take part in this study.

Signature: (Researcher): _____

Name: Adriana de Souza Crespo

Date: _____

Printed by Books on Demand GmbH, Norderstedt / Germany